>TOURIST

Greater Than a Tourist Book Series Reviews from Readers

I think the series is wonderful and beneficial for tourists to get information before visiting the city.

-Seckin Zumbul, Izmir Turkey

I am a world traveler who has read many trip guides but this one really made a difference for me. I would call it a heartfelt creation of a local guide expert instead of just a guide.

-Susy, Isla Holbox, Mexico

New to the area like me, this is a must have!

-Joe, Bloomington, USA

This is a good series that gets down to it when looking for things to do at your destination without having to read a novel for just a few ideas.

-Rachel, Monterey, USA

Good information to have to plan my trip to this destination.

-Pennie Farrell, Mexico

Aptly titled, you won't just be a tourist after reading this book. You'll be greater than a tourist!

-Alan Warner, Grand Rapids, USA

Thank you for a fantastic book.

-Don, Philadelphia, USA

Micheline Logan

Great ideas for a perfect day.
-Mary Martin USA

Even though I only have three days to spend in San Miguel in an upcoming visit, I will use the author's suggestions to guide some of my time there. An easy read - with chapters named to guide me in directions I want to go.
-Robert Catapano, USA

Great insights from a local perspective! Useful information and a very good value!
-Sarah, USA

This series provides an in-depth experience through the eyes of a local. Reading these series will help you to travel the city in with confidence and it'll make your journey a unique one.
-Andrew Teoh, Ipoh, Malaysia

Tourists can get an amazing "insider scoop" about a lot of places from all over the world. While reading, you can feel how much love the writer put in it.
-Vanja Živković, Sremski Karlovci, Serbia

GREATER THAN A TOURIST – JOHANNESBURG GAUTENG SOUTH AFRICA

50 Travel Tips from a Local

Micheline Logan

Michelle Logan

Greater Than a Tourist- Johannesburg Gauteng South Africa Copyright © 2018 by CZYK Publishing LLC. All Rights Reserved.

All rights reserved. No part of this book may be reproduced in any form or by any electronic or mechanical means including information storage and retrieval systems, without permission in writing from the author. The only exception is by a reviewer, who may quote short excerpts in a review.

Cover Images: https://pixabay.com/en/johannesburg-rpa-south-africa-city-436018/
https://pixabay.com/en/sand-dune-background-nature-desert-2848098/

Greater Than a Tourist
Visit our website at www.GreaterThanaTourist.com

Lock Haven, PA
All rights reserved.

ISBN: 9781977003379

Micheline Logan

BOOK DESCRIPTION

Are you excited about planning your next trip?

Do you want to try something new?

Would you like some guidance from a local?

If you answered yes to any of these questions, then this Greater Than a Tourist book is for you.

Greater Than a Tourist- Johannesburg Gauteng South Africa by Micheline Logan offers the inside scoop on Johannesburg. Most travel books tell you how to travel like a tourist. Although there is nothing wrong with that, as part of the Greater Than a Tourist series, this book will give you travel tips from someone who has lived at your next travel destination.

In these pages, you will discover advice that will help you throughout your stay. This book will not tell you exact addresses or store hours but instead will give you excitement and knowledge from a local that you may not find in other smaller print travel books.

Travel like a local. Slow down, stay in one place, and get to know the people and the culture. By the time you finish this book, you will be eager and prepared to travel to your next destination.

Micheline Logan

TABLE OF CONTENTS

BOOK DESCRIPTION vii
TABLE OF CONTENTS ix
DEDICATION 1
ABOUT THE AUTHOR 3
HOW TO USE THIS BOOK 5
FROM THE PUBLISHER 7
OUR STORY 9
WELCOME TO 11
> TOURIST 11
INTRODUCTION 13
  1. Some Interesting Facts about Joburg 15
  2. Getting Around Joburg 16
  3. Not much time? 16
  Take a Bus 16
  4. Those Ten Million Trees 17
  5. The Zoo and Zoo Lake 18
  6. Emmarentia and Louw Geldenhuys 19
  7. Melville Koppies 20
  8. Klipriviersberg Nature Reserve 21
  9. Take a Walk on the Wilds Side 22
  10. Feeling Peckish? Neighbourgoods. 23

11. Origins Centre Museum..24
12. Have Your DNA Analysed..24
13. The Cradle of Mankind - Maropeng...25
14. Sterkfontein Caves...26
15. Gilroy's Pub and Restaurant...26
16. Carnivore Restaurant 27
17. Nirox Park...28
18. Walter Sisulu Botanical Gardens..28
19. Montecasino Bird Gardens 29
20. Il Teatro at Montecasino 30
21. Mahatma Gandhi and Johannesburg...31
22. Constitution Hill 32
23. Liliesleaf Farm..32
24. Apartheid Museum 33
25. Gold Reef City...33
26. City Bus Tour 34
to Soweto 34
27. FNB Stadium (Soccer City)...35
28. Vilakazi Street 35
29. Bungee Jump off a Cooling Tower...36
30. Hector Pieterson Memorial..37
31. World of Beer 38
32. The Market Theatre 38
33. Museum Africa 39

34. Food; Eat a	40
Bunny chow	40
35. Maboneng	40
36. James Hall Transport Museum	41
37. Eat Some Piri-Piri	42
38. La Parreirinha	42
39. Nando's	43
40. Ascot Pharmacy	44
41. 44 Stanley Street, Melville	45
42. Bean There	46
43. 27 Boxes	46
44. Shopping: Rosebank Sunday Market	47
45. Shopping: Hyde Park	48
46. Watch a Cricket Match	49
47. Watch a Rugby Match	49
48. Watch a Soccer Match	50
49. Go for a Swim	51
50. Enter a Sporting Event	51
Top Reasons to Book This Trip	53
> TOURIST	55
GREATER THAN A TOURIST	55
> TOURIST	57
GREATER THAN A TOURIST	57
NOTES	59

Micheline Logan

DEDICATION

This book is dedicated to my friend Fabienne, who refuses to let cancer get the better of her. Wishing her many more years.

Micheline Logan

ABOUT THE AUTHOR

Micheline is a silver surfer who lives in Johannesburg. She loves the outdoors and wildlife, especially birdwatching, which makes South Africa a great place to live.

Micheline is widely travelled: Her father was in the Royal Airforce, and by the time she was eight, she had crossed the equator by sea three times. She has travelled to South America, the US, Europe, the Middle East, Australia and Asia, and, of course in Africa.

One of her other interests is open-water swimming, which has taken her to the Greek Islands, Turkey and the Red Sea.

While she loves to experience the world, she is always happy to come home to Johannesburg, where she lives and works. One thing about Jozi - it's never boring!

Micheline Logan

HOW TO USE THIS BOOK

The Greater Than a Tourist book series was written by someone who has lived in an area for over three months. The goal of this book is to help travelers either dream or experience different locations by providing opinions from a local. The author has made suggestions based on their own experiences. Please do your own research before traveling to the area in case the suggested places are unavailable.

Micheline Logan

FROM THE PUBLISHER

Traveling can be one of the most important parts of a person's life. The anticipation and memories that you have are some of the best. As a publisher of the Greater Than a Tourist book series, as well as the popular 50 Things to Know book series, we strive to help you learn about new places, spark your imagination, and inspire you. Wherever you are and whatever you do I wish you safe, fun, and inspiring travel.

Lisa Rusczyk Ed. D.
CZYK Publishing

Micheline Logan

OUR STORY

Traveling is a passion of the "Greater than a Tourist" series creator. Lisa studied abroad in college, and for their honeymoon Lisa and her husband toured Europe. During her travels to Malta, an older man tried to give her some advice based on his own experience living on the island since he was a young boy. She was not sure if she should talk to the stranger but was interested in his advice. When traveling to some places she was wary to talk to locals because she was afraid that they weren't being genuine. Through her travels, Lisa learned how much locals had to share with tourists. Lisa created the "Greater Than a Tourist" book series to help connect people with locals. A topic that locals are very passionate about sharing.

Micheline Logan

WELCOME TO
> TOURIST

Micheline Logan

INTRODUCTION

Quote about travel here. Can be from famous person or general travel quote. Please add reference

Many tourists to South Africa land at O R Tambo Airport near Johannesburg en route to other destinations such as Cape Town, Durban or the Kruger National Park. Joburg (as we know it) is perceived as a commercial capital where people go to do business and little else. This is a pity, because Joburg, Jozi or Egoli has so much to offer. Although Joburg is less than 200 years old, our ancestors have been living in its vicinity since man started walking on two legs - their past is still being unearthed. We made some wrong turns along the way, and the legacy of apartheid is recorded for you to see as well. If you are a daredevil, you can bungee-jump off a cooling tower; if you like shopping you can visit our markets, unless you are into shopping malls, of which there are plenty.

Maybe you do not have the time to visit one of our major game reserves; don't worry, we have nature reserves in and around Johannesburg that will give you a taste of Africa (and bring you back again).

Micheline Logan

There is no particular order to the tips here, except that I start off with rather laid-back places to visit and stroll around. While you won't get altitude sickness in Joburg, the thin air may make you quite tired for a day or two, so take it easy in the beginning, by visiting one or two of our open spaces to acclimatize.

You could spend a year in Joburg and not get to see and do everything, I have included some of my favourites here, but there are other attractions. The challenge is not what to experience, it is what to miss out on. Hopefully you will return again and again!

1. SOME INTERESTING FACTS ABOUT JOBURG

Johannesburg is also known as Joburg (which is a branded name for the city), Jozi, and Egoli. Egoli means "City of Gold", referring to Joburg's early days as a mining camp.

Johannesburg's altitude is almost 1800 metres above sea level. Water boils at $98_\circ$C. By the way, Joburg tap water is safe to drink.

Johannesburg is the world's largest landlocked city - it does not have a major river or lake and is hundreds of kilometres from the sea. Strangely enough, despite the lack of water, it is a port city - the largest inland port in Africa.

Although there are no major rivers, two streams are found on either side of the Witwatersrand, a rocky ridge just north of the city centre and the continental watershed. All the rain that falls south of the ridge flows into the Atlantic via the Vaal and Orange River; the rain that falls north of the ridge flows via the Limpopo into the Indian Ocean.

What it lacks in water, Joburg makes up for in trees. There are an estimated 10 million trees planted in Joburg, making it one of the world's largest man-made urban forests.

2. GETTING AROUND JOBURG

Johannesburg is a large and sprawling metropolis and, while there is public transport, it is easiest to get around either by self-drive with a hire car and a GPS or using a taxi. South African cars are right-hand-drive and the roads are generally good, but you need to be quite an assertive driver to cope with the local drivers, especially minibus taxis. Fuel is quite expensive, and like most cities, rush hour is to be avoided (6am-8am and 4pm-6:30pm).

Like most cities, Uber is alive and well and at your bid and call. If you are pressed for time, there is a tourist bus that has a selection of routes that gives you lots of bang for your buck.

3. NOT MUCH TIME? TAKE A BUS

If you are pressed for time and have only a day or two to spend sightseeing, the City Bus Sightseeing tours are a great option. These tours, done in either an open-top double-decker, or a 16 seater minibus, are an ideal way to see Joburg and many of the sights mentioned here. The bus logo indicates if an attraction is on the bus route. You buy a ticket for the route and can hop off and on at any of the destinations en route. There is a city route, that includes Constitutional Hill and Gold Reef City, a route that takes you through some of Joburg's suburbs, and a Soweto route, which can be combined with the city route.

4. THOSE TEN MILLION TREES

Stand on a high point in Johannesburg, like Northcliff or Parktown and you will see greenery stretching out everywhere. Johannesburg is actually a grassland biome with few trees, but a tradition of planting trees by early settlers has continued to this day. One of the early attempts was Sachsenwald Forest, planted by Hermann Eckstein at the turn of the nineteenth century as a timber plantation. The name was later anglicised to Saxonwold, one of the upmarket suburbs of modern-day Johannesburg.

If you visit in October, you will be treated to the sight of thousands of Jacarandas in bloom. This Brazilian import cloaks the city in mauve, and is a Japanese tourist attraction. Many Japanese visit Johannesburg and Pretoria at this time and wear clothes that match the marvellous blossoms. Exams fall soon after October, and there is a superstition that you will pass your exams if a blossom falls on you.

5. THE ZOO AND ZOO LAKE

On the border of Saxonwold lies the Johannesburg Zoo and the Zoo Lake. This land was also part of Hermann Eckstein's farm Braamfontein. After his death, in 1903, his business partners bequeathed 200 acres to Johannesburg for the recreational use of everyone who lived in Johannesburg. A small zoo was started, with the first animals being donated by Sir Percy Fitzpatrick (most famous for his book "Jock of the Bushveld" about his beloved dog). An artificial lake was constructed soon afterwards, and to this day, people of all colours and creeds enjoy walking, picknicking and boating around the Lake.

The Zoo is large (140 acres) and has some rare animals such as white lion, bongo antelope and Lord Derby Eland. Both the zoo and the Zoo lake are very busy on weekends, but fairly quiet during the week.

6. EMMARENTIA AND LOUW GELDENHUYS

Joburg was an interesting mix of gold mining and farms. Like Hermann Eckstein who was both a mining magnate and a farmer, the Geldenhuys family had a large farm and also prospected for gold. These were exciting times - between 1885 and 1895, the population of Joburg grew from 2 000 to 100 000 because of the gold rush.

Following the Anglo-Boer War, when many able men were out of work, Louw Geldenhuys commissioned the Emmarentia Dam (named after his wife). This dam provided irrigation for farms which he parcelled out and is another favourite recreation spot for Joburgers, although it is now surrounded by suburbs. If you drive along Greenfield road, you can still see Louw Geldenhuys' farmhouse, which is a beautifully maintained and privately owned heritage building. It typically has a "stoep" (verandah) around the building and there are impressive palms in the garden. A few hundred metres further on is Marks Park Sports and recreation centre, where his brother Frans' house is now the clubhouse.

Emmarentia Dam has a botanical garden adjacent to it, as well as a park where dog lovers can let their dogs run free and have a great time.

Micheline Logan

At the top of the Emmarentia Ridge is Melville Koppies, which can be visited on the weekends and holds more clues to Joburg's past.

7. MELVILLE KOPPIES

Melville Koppies (hills) lies just across the road from Marks Park, and people have been living there for at least the last 250 000 years. The original inhabitants were stone age men and Khoisan people who were probably displaced by Iron Age nomadic Setswana, based on remains of iron smelting pits found on the koppies.

The rise of the Zulu nation created great disruptions in the 1820s and the inhabitants of Melville Koppies and other communities were in turn displaced by the turmoil.

Wits University runs educational walks, both about the history and the fauna and flora of the koppies on weekends, which is when the public have access to this spot. From the top of the ridge, you can get a great view of Johannesburg and what was the original Braamfontein farm.

8. KLIPRIVIERSBERG NATURE RESERVE

Want to see wildlife but you don't have enough time to get to any of our great game reserves? Klipriviersberg is just a few kilometres from the city centre where you can get a first-hand experience of the South African veld and maybe see some antelope and zebra.

People have lived in these valleys long before Joburg came to be. Daily entrance to the reserve is free, with occasional organised walks, which you can join for a small fee, which goes towards maintaining the reserve. They usually include a slap-up breakfast.

You can spend a whole day traversing the many trails in the Reserve. Some are on level ground, others are quite challenging. Apart from wildlife such as blesbok or wildebeest, there is good birding, with lovely birds like white-fronted bee-eaters. Take your binoculars!

The main entrance is in Peggy Vera Road in Kibler Park, with secure parking.

Micheline Logan

9. TAKE A WALK ON THE WILDS SIDE

The Randlords were a group of personalities and founders of mining companies in the early days of Joburg. While they lived in great luxury in their magnificent mansions, some of which can still be seen, they also were mindful of the citizens of Johannesburg. Like Hermann Eckstein, the colourful Barney Barnato left open parkland to be used in perpetuity by the people of Joburg. Dating from 1925, the Wilds are copiously forested and many specimens of indigenous plants grow here. The Park became unsafe about twenty years ago, and people stopped visiting, but it now has a renaissance. Artist James Delaney, who lives near the Wilds has installed an Owl Garden with over 60 owl statues. People started coming back and it is becoming a popular venue again.

>TOURIST

10. FEELING PECKISH? NEIGHBOURGOODS.

Every Saturday, the commercial suburb of Braamfontein hosts Neighbourgoods, a food market with cuisines to satisfy every palate. Artisanal breads, handcrafted beers and food from all over the world (don't miss the paella!).

On the rooftop there is live entertainment and a few bars.

There are also some craft stalls which might just have those gifts you want to take back home.

Parking can be an issue, so you can take an Uber, or visit via a hop-on hop-off City sightseeing bus.

Neighbourgoods is open from 09:00 - 15:00.

"All roads lead to Johannesburg"
Alan Paton, author of "Cry the Beloved Country"

Micheline Logan

11. ORIGINS CENTRE MUSEUM

Also situated in Braamfontein is the Origins Centre Museum of Witwatersrand University, less than 2 kilometres from Neighbourgoods and open from Monday to Saturday. This fascinating museum explores our earliest beginnings and has an extensive collection of early tools and rock art.

There is also comprehensive information about the San (Bushman) tribes and their culture, from which we could take some lessons in how to live and share.

Well worth a visit for a couple of hours. If you are feeling adventurous, you can get your DNA tested here.

12. HAVE YOUR DNA ANALYSED

You can get your DNA tested at the Origins Museum, usually on the first Saturday of each month. You will need to book in advance, as the event is limited to 60 guests. Presentations about evolution and genetic ancestry are given, and you can either just sign up for the talks or opt for DNA testing as well. The test results take about 8-14 weeks to be completed (the quick turnaround on DNA testing you see on TV is strictly fiction) and can be posted to you on completion. Please refer to the Origins Museum website for pricing and to download the application form.

13. THE CRADLE OF MANKIND - MAROPENG

If you enjoyed Origins, you must not miss Maropeng in the "Cradle of Humankind". This World Heritage site north-west of Johannesburg is famous for the number of remains of very early hominids found in the various caves in the region, like "Mrs Ples" and "Little Foot". Over 40% of the world's hominid fossils have been found here, truly justifying the name of "Cradle of Humankind".

Maropeng is a museum built to house some of these finds and depicts the history of our earliest forefathers. The museum is built in the form of a tumulus (burial mound) and starts our story with the first emergence of life on our planet.

You can combine this with a visit to one of the caves where these archaeological finds have been made, if you are not claustrophobic, the Sterkfontein Caves.

14. STERKFONTEIN CAVES

This is where many of the remains displayed at Maropeng were discovered. The Sterkfontein Caves have been open for viewing for nearly 100 years. The presence of fossils was first noted by miners in the 1890s. They were mining the caves for limestone. Raymond Dart and Robert Broom started an archaeological dig in the 1930s with their students from the University of the Witwatersrand, which is still in progress today.

While the mining probably destroyed hundreds of fossils, about 500 hominids have been identified, as well as many mammals, some of which are extinct today.

The caves are quite cool as you walk through them. Some openings are a bit narrow, but it is an exhilarating trip to combine with Maropeng.

15. GILROY'S PUB AND RESTAURANT

While there are quite a few venues where you can have a meal in the vicinity of Maropeng, Gilroy's Pub offers some light entertainment after your educational visits. Wooden benches and tables are set around a roomy courtyard where reasonably priced and tasty pub grub is served, such as fish and chips, pies, and other hearty fare. There are salads and some fusion food too, which you can accompany with one of Gilroy's craft beers.

On the weekends there will be one or more artists singing for their supper, usually with a folk/Irish flavour. A great place to relax for all ages. There are also a few shops selling goodies such as handmade soaps, African curios and other items to add to your luggage.

16. CARNIVORE RESTAURANT

You may have heard of the original Carnivore restaurant in Nairobi. This is the South African franchise, where you can eat conventional dishes, both carnivorous and vegetarian, or you can opt to eat some flesh you have not tried before, like crocodile, ostrich and other African game. You can eat as much as you like, and admit defeat by lowering the flag on your table; until you do this, the waiters will bring you more and more to eat.

There is also a kiddies' menu available. The meat is cooked on an open fire, you might call it a barbecue; we South Africans call it a braai or braaivleis, literally "roasted meat".

17. NIROX PARK

Based in the area of the Cradle of Humankind, Nirox park is a 15-hectare artists' park, with sculptures strategically placed in the gardens. Some of the artists reside and work in the park.

The park is open from 10-17:00 on weekends to the public. A private visit can be arranged by contacting Nirox, where you can visit the artist's studios by previous arrangement.

Occasional events and concerts are held, notably a festival in winter, when various eating establishments from the Cape come and set up pop-up food stalls. This is a very popular event and tickets have to be booked well in advance.

With abundant ponds and dams, Nirox is a tranquil haven to visit and relax.

18. WALTER SISULU BOTANICAL GARDENS

On the West Rand, these beautiful botanical gardens are a great place to chill, attend the occasional concert or look for the famous black eagles that nest on the cliff over the waterfall (There is another pair near Klipriviersberg, but they are not so easy to see). You can bring your own picnic or buy food at the tea-room and restaurant.

These gardens were officially opened in the 1980s, but have been enjoyed by generations before then. There is a bird hide adjoining a small dam and special botanical sections for cycads, ferns, aloes, ethnobotanical plants and other examples of South Africa's floral kingdoms.

19. MONTECASINO BIRD GARDENS

While Montecasino is a casino in the North of Johannesburg, it also has other attractions, such as the Bird Gardens. This is a pleasant spot with walk-through aviaries housing local and exotic bird species. In addition, there is a show held 2-3 times a day, where birds interact with their keepers and the audience. The birds perform "acts", based on their natural behaviour, such as a crow that picks up tin cans. It can be quite impressive having a Eurasian Eagle Owl or a White-backed Vulture flying just over your head when you are sitting in the small ampitheatre!

In addition to birds, there are a few mammals, such as lemurs and meerkats, reptile exhibits and a small collection of frogs and spiders. There is also a pleasant tea-room called the Flamingo, where you can relax.

Micheline Logan

20. IL TEATRO AT MONTECASINO

The Theatre at Montecasino can stage large-scale events and has hosted fabulous shows like the "Lion King" and "West Side Story". The quality and energy of these shows is world-class.

Check up if there are any shows on that take your fancy.

There are many places to eat inside the casino and theatre complex, including fish restaurants and Italian. There are venues for the whole family, apart from the Bird garden, such as a bowling alley, movies and a kid's entertainment section. There is even a creche.

"I learnt during all those years to love Johannesburg, even though it was a mining camp. It was in Johannesburg that I found my most precious friends. It was in Johannesburg that the foundation for the great struggle of Passive Resistance was laid... Johannesburg, therefore had the holiest of all the holy assocation that Mrs Gandhi and I will carry back to India"

– Mohandas Gandhi, 1914

21. MAHATMA GANDHI AND JOHANNESBURG

Many South Africans are unaware what a major part South Africa, and Johannesburg, played in the Mahatma's life. There is a museum at Satyagraha House in Orchards.

This is where Gandhi formulated the concept of passive resistance or "satyagraha" when he stayed here in 1908-9 with his close friend, Hermann Kallenbach, an architect, who designed the house.

You can also stay at Satyagraha House, but it is not budget accommodation.

There are other sites in Johannesburg that commemorate Gandhi and there is a specialist tour that can take you round to all the places, if you wish. When you visit Constitution Hill, you will be reminded that Gandhi was imprisoned there, like so many other important figures of South African history.

22. CONSTITUTION HILL

This is one of the must-sees of your trip. Formerly a fort during the Anglo-Boer war and a notorious prison, this building on Braamfontein's ridge is now the site of South Africa's Constitutional Court, where disputes around constitutional matters are judged.

While thousands of prisoners spent their time here, we remember Mahatma Gandhi, Nelson Mandela, Albert Luthuli, Robert Sobukwe, Winnie Mandela, Albertina Sisulu and Fatima Meer as some of the inmates. The prisons they were held in can be visited.

There is also a comprehensive art collection that started on a shoestring budget and expanded dramatically, including woks from renowned artists such as Marc Chagall and William Kentridge.

23. LILIESLEAF FARM

Liliesleaf Farm in Rivonia was a sanctuary for the South African Communist party and the liberation movement and most of the key figures stayed or met here, including Nelson Mandela and Walter Sisulu.

Visitors to the heritage site can watch an audiovisual presentation of the history and times of the place and the people and see museum exhibits. The proceedings of the Rivonia trial were based on the people who were arrested at Liliesleaf.

24. APARTHEID MUSEUM

A must-visit experience to try and understand the lunacy that was apartheid. The architectural design was inspired by the content and has many symbols integrated into the building.

When you visit the museum, it is an experiental pilgrimage that enables you to understand what life was like living under apartheid if your skin was not white. The classifications were arbitrary: Chinese were regarded as "black", while Japanese were "honorary whites" because of the trade South Africa did with Japan.

Children under 12 are not admitted to the museum because of the graphic imagery contained there.

25. GOLD REEF CITY

You might think it odd to write about the Apartheid Museum and then about a casino and theme park, but the fact of the matter is that the Apartheid Museum is right next door to Gold Reef City, and it was built by the Casino consortium as a contribution to society.

While it is a theme park and has fun rides, Gold Reef City is built over an actual mine and one can experience some of the mining experience; taking the lift down to a mining stope, watching gold being poured and panning for gold.

Micheline Logan

Apart from the gold mining history and the fun rides, there is even a Victorian chapel that was originally built for the miners of Joburg. This chapel has been moved, brick by brick to the current site and can be used as a wedding venue.

26. CITY BUS TOUR TO SOWETO

There are many sights to see in Soweto (this exotic name is actually an abbreviation of South-West Township) and the best way to experience them is via a guided tour or the City Bus Sightseeing Soweto extension, which can be combined with the Red Bus tour. The starting point for the tour is at the Apartheid museum, where the Red Bus tour will drop you off. Alternatively you can arrange one of the many guided tours through your hotel or other accommodation.

There are also biking tours for the more athletically inclined.

You should visit the main tourist spots, as well as stop at some of the famous eateries, such as Sakhumzi's en route, starting with the FNB Stadium

27. FNB STADIUM (SOCCER CITY)

When South Africa won the opportunity to host the Fifa Soccer World Cup in 2010, although there were stadiums in the main cities and towns, many of them needed revamping to cater for the huge crowds that would fill them. Soccer city (now known as the FNB Stadium) was rebuilt in the form of a giant calabash and is the largest stadium in Africa.

You can take a guided tour of the stadium, or even better, you can attend a soccer match or even a concert if the timing is right. Performers as diverse as Santana and Lady Gaga have performed here.

28. VILAKAZI STREET

Famous for being the only street on the planet where two Nobel laureates lived, Vilakazi Street is now lined with places to eat and shop. The two laureates are Nelson Mandela and Desmond Tutu, who still shares his time between his home in Cape Town and his simple house on Vilakazi Street.

Mandela's house is now a small museum, which takes about 15 minutes to see.

You can browse the shops for local handcrafts and try some township cuisine at Sakhumzi or one of the other spots after visiting the museum. There is also a container shop called the Box Shop which contains a roastery called Kofi and a design store.

29. BUNGEE JUMP OFF A COOLING TOWER

For the daredevil in you, here is an opportunity to bungee jump under controlled conditions. The jump takes place between the two vibrantly painted towers.

You do not have to bungee off these cooling towers, the remnants of an old power station, you can just get to the top and have a great view. There is a Chisanyama (grilled meat) restaurant at the base of the towers. If you take one of the Soweto bicycle tours or the bus tour, the cooling towers are part of the route.

30. HECTOR PIETERSON MEMORIAL

Hector Pieterson was a 12-year old who was shot dead by a policeman in the June 1976 Soweto Uprising. Children from Soweto took to the streets to protest against learning Afrikaans at school. Hector was one of the first casualties.

Two blocks from the memorial there is a museum dedicated to him and those dark times. It explains the problems of the segregated education of the time, and why the children protested. The reaction of the police that day was totally out of proportion and brutal.

"No one is born hating another person because of the colour of his skin, or his background, or his religion. People must learn to hate, and if they can learn to hate, they can be taught to love, for love comes more naturally to the human heart than its opposite." - Nelson Mandela - Long Walk to Freedom.

31. WORLD OF BEER

The Newtown Precinct, which can be accessed via the City Bus sightseeing red Route, is one of the oldest parts of Joburg and has many attractions for a day tour.

The World of Beer is a museum to the world's oldest brew, and was established by South African Breweries, which became SAB-Miller and is now merged with Anheuser-Busch.

This is a very enjoyable tour, where you learn about the brewing of beer and can indulge in some beer-tasting. One Saturday a month is dedicated to a beer and food pairing experience, where different beers are matched with suitable dishes. There is a good restaurant and even a souvenir shop selling SAB branded goods.

32. THE MARKET THEATRE

Newtown was the original home of Joburg's Market, and many of the buildings date back to that time. The Market Theatre was the old Indian Fruit market.

Started in 1976 by Barney Simon and Mannie Manim, this theatre became synonymous with struggle politics and theatre expressing anti-regime sentiments. Some of South Africa's greatest playwrights and their plays were first showcased here, including Athol Fugard, William

Kentridge and the Handspring Puppet Company. The last-named fabricated the stunning "War Horse" for the play of the same name. If you cannot get to see a show, consider the guided tour through the theatres, which takes about 90 minutes.

33. MUSEUM AFRICA

Housed in the Old Market together with the Market Theatre in Newtown, Museum Africa is a social and cultural history museum, predominantly about Johannesburg. The collection holds over 850 000 items, only a few of which can be on display at one time.

With artefacts ranging from Ancient Egyptian and Ethiopian art to implements of daily life in the mining town of Joburg, Museum Africa is constantly evolving.

You can also take a tour of the Newtown Precinct, which has other attractions, such as the Sci-Bono Centre and the Bassline, a legendary club where artists such as Abdullah Ibrahim started their careers.

Micheline Logan

34. FOOD; EAT A BUNNY CHOW

To be truthful, the home of Bunny chow is Durban, but that does not mean you cannot sample one in Joburg. No it is not a salad, nor does it include any rabbit. It is half a loaf of bread hollowed out and filled with a tasty curry - the ultimate street food.

While the best bunny chow is reputed to be had at "Curry and All" in Sandton, you can try your first chow at places like Neighbourgoods.

Why is it called bunny chow? No-one is really sure, although at one time Indians were known as "Banya" and "chow" is slang for food. By the way, Durban has the largest Indian population of any city outside India.

35. MABONENG

Maboneng Precinct is a regeneration project of the inner city. Housed in what was once a run-down and unsafe part of the city, this is now a hot spot to visit and even live.

Maboneng ("Place of Light" in Sesotho) is a hub for creatives, and you can visit their boutiques interspersed with eateries offering everything from Mexican to Ethiopian food.

There are many events on the go, including the Thursday night cycling tour, where cyclists take to the streets of Joburg in the vicinity of Maboneng.

The City Bus Red Route has a stop here.

36. JAMES HALL TRANSPORT MUSEUM

Also visited by the City Bus Red Route is the James Hall Museum in the South of Joburg. Definitely a place for boys and their toys, over 400 years of transport is represented in this collection assembled by James Hall, starting with vehicles pulled by animals and graduating through to motor vehicles that we are more familiar with.

There are bicycles and motorbikes, including the penny-farthing and some very rare and special sedans, as well as steam driven vehicles and tractors.

The Portuguese restaurant La Parreirinha is less than a kilometre away, if you get peckish for piri-piri prawns.

37. EAT SOME PIRI-PIRI

South African cuisine is very diverse because of the many cultures that populated the country, either voluntarily or involuntarily. Slaves from Indonesia adapted their cuisine to fit the ingredients available, resulting in Cape Malay cooking. Indian, French and Dutch food also contributed to the mix, and there are some unique South African flavours based on the botanical treasure-house of the Cape, such as Rooibos tea. One cuisine that has made a strong impression is Portuguese-African cooking, especially piri-piri sauce. Piri-piri is a chili sauce and there are many varieties, ranging from hot to incendiary. If you are not familiar with this sauce, you must try prawns or cooked with it. For those who are not addicted to chili, there are softer options, such as lemon and herb. There are many places to eat Portuguese, we will just mention two.

38. LA PARREIRINHA

You will probably need to take a taxi to find this restaurant (pronounce it "Pa-Ray-ring-ya"!), buried in the heart of South Johannesburg. It is located in an old police station and has been going strong for around fifty years. It is definitely not posh, but the quality of the food is renowned.

Apart from Piri-piri prawns and chicken, you can also feast on caldo verde, the famous vegetable soup, trinchado, a hearty beef stew and finish off with natas, small custard tarts. Wash it all down with a mozambican beer.

There may be posher eateries that serve Portuguese fare, but they do not have the ambience of this spot. The ceiling is festooned with thousands of ties left behind after expansive business lunches. If you cannot get a booking, they have recently opened a fast food outlet nearby, ask where the "Rapido" is situated.

39. NANDO'S

Another Portuguese eatery just up the road from La Parreirinha is the original Nando's, a nondescript takeaway joint, which now has branches all over the world. You may be familiar with Nando's if you come from Britain, but if not we suggest you try a take-away from them (although they also have tables).

Nando's have won their loyal clientele both by consistent service and products and by their irreverent humour. if there is some political happening, Nando's will have something cheeky to say about it. Sometimes some of their ads have been banned from TV broadcasts, but fortunately you can view them on Youtube.

Micheline Logan

40. ASCOT PHARMACY

We know how it is; there is always at least one person for whom you have to buy perfume or after-shave when you travel. While this does give you something to do at "duty-free" during the wait to board your plane, consider a trip to Ascot Pharmacy. This very unimposing shop sells a wide range of perfumes, a fact you will find hard to believe when you visit it. Do not go around Valentine's Day, Mother's Day or Christmas, as the shop is packed to capacity then.

You will find that the prices are very competitive and often better than the duty-free shops, because of their low overheads and huge volumes that they sell. They also have an online store if you are staying long enough to take a delivery.

Working in South Africa and the people in Johannesburg get under your skin. It stays with you. It's a place I want to take my children back to. It's a place that filled me with great joy and inspiration but also sadness. I think it's one of the most complex places on the planet.
-Ryan Phillippe

41. 44 STANLEY STREET, MELVILLE

Melville has been a trendy and bohemian suburb for ovr 60 years, and 44 Stanley is typical of the suburb. From the outside it is a rather bleak industrial building, but enter the courtyards within and prepare to be enchanted.

There are interesting shops and boutiques, interspersed with laid-back places to eat and drink. A few of the places you can find here include:-

Lucky Fish - the modern equivalent of a trading store

L'Elephant Terrible Bookshop

The Salvation Café - for breakfast and lunch

Il Giardino - Italian food among the olive trees

Black Coffee - fashion design

But we recommend you just go and visit and do your own exploring.

42. BEAN THERE

One of the shops at 44 Stanley is Bean There, a coffee roastery. Their main business is importing fair trade coffee for upmarket game lodges and hotels, and you can sample some of the roasts they produce. Try Ethiopian beans, the origin of all coffees and naturally low in caffeine.

Apart from the fact that the beans are really freshly ground, sipping coffee while beans are roasting near you enhances the flavour. Cake is served to stave off those hunger pangs.

If you are not much of a coffee drinker, Lady Bonin's Tea is the place for you, they craft teas from organic ingredients. If it is a cold day, why not pop into Chocoloza and have a hot chocolate, while deciding which handcrafted chocolates you want to buy.

43. 27 BOXES

Also in Melville, a few km away from 44 Stanley is 27 Boxes, a collection of containers housing pop-up and permanent shops that always have something new and entertaining. Fashion and interior design are prominently featured, and there is artisanal bread and other goodies for the food lover.

44. SHOPPING: ROSEBANK SUNDAY MARKET

The Rosebank Sunday market is the place to buy all your gifts to take home with you. Based in the roof parking of the Rosebank Mall, you can buy goods ranging from pewter and porcelain to African curios from West Africa.

There are many artists who have their works on display and are quite used to either sending their work to your home or packaging it to take with you on your flight home.

There are also food stalls selling everything from artisanal bread to Malay curries.

If you cannot make the Sunday Market, the curio sellers operate during the week from outside the front of the Mall.

There is also good shopping and eating in Rosebank, which is a conglomeration of malls and arcades. There is a Gautrain station in Rosebank, from where you can embark for Pretoria or O R Tambo Airport.

Micheline Logan

45. SHOPPING: HYDE PARK

Hyde Park is by no means the largest mall in Joburg, but it is where the well-heeled shop. The biggest branch of the Exclusive Books chain is found here and you can browse there for some books to add to your baggage allowance.

Hyde Park is the oldest free-standing shopping centre in Joburg, but it has gone through a series of revamps to stay contemporary. It is smaller and more compact than nearby Sandton City, and not so frenetic.

You can buy the best of European fashion, beautiful jewellery and new luggage if you are tired of your current baggage. There is also a cinema complex.

The concierge service at the Centre will arrange transport for you if you contact them.

46. WATCH A CRICKET MATCH

It does not matter if you do not understand the first thing about cricket; a day at the Wanderers watching a match is still a lot of fun, even if it is only in watching the antics of the crowd.

The Wanderers Stadium is known as the "Bull Run" and has been home to many international cricket matches.

Remember to take lots of sun-block and a hat. If you know someone who understands cricket, take them with you to explain what a googly, a wide and a no-ball are.

47. WATCH A RUGBY MATCH

South Africa is a sport-loving nation - in summer, there is cricket and football. In winter there is rugby. Book for a match to be played at Ellis Park (now known as Emirates Airline Park). Whether it is an international or a local fixture does not matter, you will get to sit among local supporters and inhale the vibe.

48. WATCH A SOCCER MATCH

We already mentioned the FNB Stadium. Try and watch a football match if there is one scheduled. Get familiar with the main teams, there are many, but the main two are Orlando Pirates and Kaizer Chiefs (no, the rock band borrowed the name). Pirates are also known as the Bucs or Buccaneers, Chiefs are also known as Amakhozi (Zulu for Chiefs). Once a year there is a match known as the Derby, a sort of Cup Final, which usually involves these teams playing each other, although Pirates have been a bit off form recently.

If you watched the Soccer World Cup in 2010, you will know what a vuvusela is - a plastic horn that emits a sound like a cow with a stomach-ache. No soccer match would be complete in South Africa without blowing a vuvu - you can get one for yourself when you enter the stadium. You will also see fans wearing makarapas - mining hats dressed up in team colours, with bits and pieces - a great souvenir.

49. GO FOR A SWIM

If you visit Joburg in summer and your accommodation does not have a pool, there are plenty of municipal pools scattered around the city (excluding Sandton). You can take a picnic lunch and laze about at the Zoo Lake pool, for instance. If you are a serious swimmer, head for Ellis Park, which is an Olympic-size pool. Most of the pools are not heated and close from April to September, except for a few. Consult the city of Joburg website for a list of pools.

50. ENTER A SPORTING EVENT

There are plenty of sporting events throughout the year, from fun runs to marathons and triathlons. There is also the famous 94.7 cycle race towards the end of the year, the only tricky part about entering it is borrowing or hiring a bike, but maybe you can find one in the Junk Mail and sell it or donate it when you leave. There are a few open water events too, between October and March.

Remember that Joburg's altitude means that there is less oxygen for your body and that you will find it harder going than at sea level.

Micheline Logan

TOP REASONS TO BOOK THIS TRIP

- **Joburg's amazing weather:** Winter runs from April to October, during which time there is virtually no rain. It can be very cold, with overnight temperatures going down to zero, but the days are clear and sunny. Summer has heavy convectional rainstorms, usually in the afternoons, which cools those hot days down.
- **The People.** While Joburg has about 5 million inhabitants, it often seems like a village. Stand in a queue anywhere, from the supermarket to a sports venue, and total strangers will open a conversation with you. South Africans are well-known for their hospitality.
- **So much to see and do.** We have left out quite a few other attractions because space does not permit. If you actually run out of sights and events in Joburg (you will need a year), head for Pretoria, which is only 80km away or a short journey on the Gautrain.

Micheline Logan

> TOURIST
GREATER THAN A TOURIST

Visit GreaterThanATourist.com:

http://GreaterThanATourist.com

Sign up for the Greater Than a Tourist Newsletter:

http://eepurl.com/cxspyf

Follow us on Facebook:

https://www.facebook.com/GreaterThanATourist

Follow us on Pinterest:

http://pinterest.com/GreaterThanATourist

Follow us on Instagram:

http://Instagram.com/GreaterThanATourist

Micheline Logan

> TOURIST
GREATER THAN A TOURIST

Please leave your honest review of this book on Amazon and Goodreads. Thank you. We appreciate your positive and constructive feedback. Thank you.

Micheline Logan

>TOURIST

NOTES

Printed in Poland
by Amazon Fulfillment
Poland Sp. z o.o., Wrocław